THE SUPREME COURT'S EXTRAORDINARY APPELLATE JURISDICTION: EXAMINING ARTICLE 136 OF THE INDIAN CONSTITUTION

VOLUME 2, ISSUE 1 OF BRAIN BOOSTER ARTICLES

NAVEEN TALAWAR

Contents

Preface

"Start writing, no matter what. The water does not flow until the faucet is turned on".

-Louis L'Amour

Hundreds of students and professors are contributing their work to Brillopedia, we are here to provide ample information about Law and Contemporary issues. Our aim is to provide a platform for today's generation to express their views and ideas on law and contemporary law.

Publication

This research paper is published in volume 2, issue 1 of Brillopedia

CHAPTER ONE

ABSTRACT

The Supreme Court is the country's highest court and the highest arbitrator, and it is primarily supposed to adjudicate on constitutional issues, hence it has been granted extraordinary jurisdiction under Article 136 of the Indian Constitution. Article 136 gives the Supreme Court very special and broad discretionary appellate jurisdiction to consider appeals from the orders and determinations of tribunals as well as courts.

In general, high court decisions can be appealed to the Supreme Court under Articles 132 to 136 of the Indian constitution, however, there may be some cases where justice and equity require the Supreme Court's intervention; in such cases, the Supreme Court has been granted extraordinary powers under Article 136 of the Indian Constitution. The Supreme Court's jurisdiction is plenary under this article, and the Constituent Assembly left it to the Supreme Court to define and delineate the province of the jurisdiction. This article aims to examine this unique appellate jurisdiction with the help of judicial decisions.

CHAPTER TWO

INTRODUCTION

Special leave petition holds the prime place in the Indian judicial system as it provides the aggrieved party special permission to be heard in the apex court in an appeal against any judgment or order of any court or tribunal in the territory of India.[1] Article 136 of the Indian constitution empowers the Supreme Court of India to grant special leave to file an appeal against[2] any judgment or order or decree in any matter or cause passed or made by any Court or Tribunal in the territory of India.[3]

The Jurisdiction of the Supreme Court under Article 136 is plenary and the Constituent Assembly has left the matter to the Supreme Court itself to define and delineate the province of the jurisdiction.[4] The power vested in the Supreme Court under Article 136 is special as it broadens the scope for invocation of the appellate jurisdiction of the Supreme Court. However, the exercise of such extraordinary power is subject to the discretion of the Supreme Court itself.

CHAPTER THREE

ORIGIN OF SPECIAL LEAVE TO APPEAL

The origin of leave to appeal can be traced back to the United Kingdom's King-in-Council, who was regarded as the last option when a situation of injustice emerged due to default or error in the lower courts' decision. The basis for such an exercise was the sovereign's royal prerogative as a fountain of justice.[1]

This prerogative has been described in England as follows:"

"....During the initial period, the petition to appeal to the King-in-Council was considered to be a matter of grace where he exercised his discretion. Later, royal charters were passed to set up Courts and allow appeals resulting in a privilege for King's subjects, but appeals could still be brought before the King-in-Council with special permission. Such appeals came to be designated 'appeals by special leave.' The appeals lay outside the conditions of limitations, which were prescribed for purposes of 'appeals as of right." [2]

Before the constitution's enactment " the privy council had the right to grant special leave from any civil or criminal action decided by any court in India.[3] However special leave to appeal in criminal cases was granted very rarely for the judicial committee.[4] This was emphasized in the case of **Arnold v. The King Emperor,**[5] where it was observed that "This Committee is not a Court of Criminal Appeal. Only when some clear departure from the requirements of justice was alleged to have taken place, and it is shown that, by a disregard of the forms of legal process, or by some violation of the principles of natural justice, or otherwise, substantial and grave injustice has been done, would the Judicial Committee interfere with the course of criminal justice."

The term "special leave" was found in the Government of India Act 1935, which included provisions for granting special leave to appeal to the privy council.[6] Section 206 of the said Act, which deals with the Federal Legislature's power to enlarge appellate jurisdiction, states that the Federal Legislature may provide by the enactment that an appeal may lie to the Federal Court in certain civil cases from a judgment, decree, or final order of a High Court, without any certification, but no appeal shall lie under any Act unless the Federal Court grants "special leave" to appeal... [7]

further, it goes on to state that if the Federal Legislature makes "such provision" as stated above then a consequential provision may also be made by the Act for abolishing, in whole or part, direct appeals in civil cases from the High Courts to His Majesty- in- Council, either with or without special leave.[8]

The framers of the constitution were aware of this legal position and have therefore included a section similar to section 206 of the 1935 Act in Clause 94(b) of the First Draft Constitution by Constitutional Advisers. The Drafting Committee later turned it into a separate Article, Article 112, in its Draft Constitution.[9]

Article 112, reads as follows; "The Supreme Court may, in its discretion, grant special leave to appeal from any judgment, decree or final order in any cause or matter, passed or made by any court or tribunal in the territory of India except the States for the time being specified in Part III of the First Schedule, in cases where the provisions of article 110 or article 111 of this Constitution do not apply.'[10]

CHAPTER FOUR

CONSTITUENT ASSEMBLY DEBATES ON SPECIAL LEAVE PETITION

On the 6th of June 1949 and the 16th of October 1949, the above-mentioned article was extensively debated.**Shri Ram Sahai proposed** an amendment to remove the words 'except the States for the time being specified in Part III of the First Schedule, in cases where the provisions of Article 110 or Article 111 of this Constitution do not apply,' which barred the Supreme Court from hearing any case on appeal from a court or tribunal of the Unions of States. He further argued that the Supreme Court should not be subjected to such jurisdictional restrictions. The Assembly overwhelmingly supported this amendment, with several members arguing in favor of an explicit expansion of the court's powers.[1]

Prof ShibbanLalSaxenasuggested that the court should be empowered to decide those appeals based on the principles of jurisprudence and considerations of natural justice

Shri Krishna Chandra Sharma supported this provision, saying, "I want this jurisdiction, which the Privy Council has enjoyed, to be enjoyed and expanded by our Court, without being limited by any canon or any provision of law."[2]

The Article was also supported by **ShriAlladiKrishnaswamiAyyar,** who clarified that the Supreme Court was free to develop its own rules when exercising its jurisdictions and that nothing prevented it from intervening even in criminal cases.

Pandit Thakur Das Bhargava was skeptical of the provision, believing it was "exceptionally broad" and a "remnant of the most accursed political prerogative of the divine right of kings," putting the Supreme Court "beyond the law." [3]

Shri H.V. Pataskar, a supporter of the Article, negated this assertion, saying that the Supreme Court is unlikely to grant special leave in any matter unless it finds that it involves a serious breach of some principle in the administration of justice or a breach of certain principles that strike at the very heart of the administration of justice between man and man. [4]

The proposed amendment was accepted by the assembly and draft Article 112 was initially adopted on 6th June 1949. **T.T Krishnamachari** then proposed replacing the Article entirely with the following: [5]

Article 112.(1) The Supreme court may, in its discretion, grant special leave to appeal from any judgment, decree, determination sentence, or order in any cause or matter passed or made by any court or tribunal in the territory of India.

(2) Nothing in clause (1) of this article shall apply to any judgment, determination, sentence or order passed or made by any court or tribunal constituted by or under any law relating to the Armed Forces.' [6]

The Assembly accepted the amendment, and on October 16, 1949, the altered Draft Article was enacted [7], giving rise to the current Article 136.

CHAPTER FIVE

SCOPE OF ARTICLE 136

Article 136 reads as follows: **Special leave to appeal by the Supreme Court,**

1. Notwithstanding anything in this Chapter, the Supreme Court may, in its discretion, grant special leave to appeal from any judgment, decree, determination, sentence, or order in any cause or matter passed or made by any court or tribunal in the territory of India

2. Nothing in clause (1) shall apply to any judgment, determination, sentence or order passed or made by any court or tribunal constituted by or under any law relating to the Armed Forces[1]

The power given to the supreme court under this provision of the Constitution is very broad and the Court has made extensive use of its prerogative power[2], The jurisdiction under Article 136 is plenary and residuary and is basically one of conscience.[3] It is sweeping power exercisable outside the purview of ordinary law to meet the pressing demands of justice.[4]

The start of the Article with a non-obstante clause itself expresses its overriding effect and indicates the intention of the framers of the Constitution of India to provide a residuary power unfettered by any statute or other provisions of the constitution. It is extraordinary in its amplitude. Its limit, when it chases injustice, is the sky.[5]

However, Article 136 does not confer any right of appeal upon the party, but it vests discretion in the Supreme Court to interfere in exceptional cases, which is to be used for furthering the ends of justice.[6] In other words, the Constitution has not made the Supreme Court a regular Court of Appeal or a Court of Error. This Court only intervenes where justice, equity, and good conscience require such intervention.[7]

In **Baiganna v. Deputy Collector of Consolidation**[8]; Krishna Iyer, J. Clearly stated;

"The Supreme Court is more than a Court of appeal. It exercises power only when there is a supreme need. It is not the fifth court of appeal but the final court of the nation. Therefore, even if legal flaws may be electronically detected, we cannot interfere sans manifest injustice or substantial question of public importance".

At the commencement of the Indian constitution, the supreme court ruled that the extraordinary power granted by Article 136 must be used only in cases where special circumstances are demonstrated. However, since 1980, the Special Leave jurisdiction has expanded significantly.

The supreme court has complete discretion over the matter, and the only limitation upon it is the "wisdom of the judges" of the court. The nature of the supreme court's power under Article 136 has been described in several cases, as follows:

The Supreme Court observed in **Pritam Singh v. The State**[9] that "the power under Art.136 must be exercised sparingly and only in exceptional cases." It was also noted that it will only exercise its jurisdiction when exceptional circumstances exist and a substantial and grave injustice has occurred.

The supreme court described its power under Art.136 as "an untrammeled reservoir of power incapable of being confined to definitional bounds" in **Kunhayamed v. State of Orissa.**[10] And the essence of the special leave petition was stated in **Narpat Singh v. Jaipur Development Authority**[11] wherein it was observed that "the exercise of the jurisdiction conferred on this Court by Article 136 of the Constitution is discretionary." It does not grant a party to the litigation the right to appeal; rather, it grants this Court broad discretionary powers to be used to meet the demands of justice. On the one hand, it is an exceptional power to be used sparingly, with caution, and with care, and to remedy extraordinary situations resulting in gross failures of justice; on the other hand, it is an overriding power through which the court may generously step in to impart justice and remedy injustice."

In **Tirupati Balaji Developers Pvt. Ltd v. State of Bihar,**[12] the Supreme Court observed "it is an extraordinary jurisdiction vested in the supreme court by the constitution with implicit trust, faith, and extraordinary care and caution has to be observed in the exercise of this jurisdiction. Article 136 does not confer the party any right of appeal but instead grants the supreme court broad discretion to be exercised based on justice, the call of duty, and eradicating injustice".

The Supreme court stated in **Delhi Judicial Service Association v. State of Gujarat,** [13] that "the court's appellate power under article 136 is plenary; it may entertain any appeal by granting special leave against any order made by any magistrate, tribunal, or other subordinate courts." As a result, this court has supervisory jurisdiction over all courts in India.

In **Jamshed Hormusji Wadia v. Board of Trustees, Port of Mumbai,** [14] it was observedthat "the supreme court's discretionary power is plenary in nature in the sense that there are no words in article 136 itself qualifying that power, and that this overriding and exceptional power has been vested in the supreme court to be exercised sparingly and only in the furtherance of the cause of justice in the supreme court in exceptional cases only."

Although Article 136 gives the Supreme Court broad discretionary powers, it is necessary for this Court to use that discretion only in cases where awards are made in violation of the principles of natural justicc, causing substantial and grave injustice to parties, or discloses such other exceptional or special circumstances that merit the Court's discretionary jurisdiction. [15]

In **Arunachalam v. Sadhanatknam,** [16] it was held that "Article 136 of the Indian Constitution gives the Supreme Court broad appellate power over all Indian courts and tribunals. However, due to the nature of the power, the Court has limited its own ability to exercise it. It is now the Court's well-established practice to allow the use of the power under Article 136 only in very exceptional circumstances, such as when a question of law of general public importance arises or a decision shocks the Court's conscience".

In **P.S.R. Sadhanantham v. Arunachalam,** [17] Justice Krishna Iyer substantiated the reasoning for limiting the scope of SLPs. [18] He said, "The wider the discretionary power, the more sparing its exercise. A number of times this Court has stressed that though parties promiscuously "provoke" this jurisdiction, the Court parsimoniously invokes the power. It is true that the strictest vigilance over abuse of the process of the court, especially at the expensively exalted level of the Supreme Court, should be maintained and ordinarily meddlesome bystanders should not be granted a "visa" [19]

In **S.G. Chemicals and Dyes Employees Union v. Management,** [20] the Supreme Court reiterated the following:

"The powers of this Court under Article 136 are very wide but as clause (1) of that Article itself states, the grant of special leave to appeal is in the discretion of the Court. Article 136 is, therefore, not designed to permit direct access to this Court where another equally efficacious remedy is available and where the question is not of public importance. Today, when the dockets of this Court are over-crowded, nay - almost choked, with the flood, or rather the avalanche, of work pouring into the Court, threatening to sweep away the present system of administration of justice itself, the Court should be extremely vigilant in exercising its discretion under Article 136."

The Supreme Court has rightly declined to limit its discretionary power by establishing principles or rules. In **Dhakeshwari Cotton Mills Ltd. v. Commissioner of Income Tax, West Bengal,**[21] the Constitutional Bench stated that it is "impossible to define with any precision the limitations on the exercise of the discretionary jurisdiction vested" in the Supreme Court under Article 136 and that the limitations "are implicit in the nature and character of the power itself." As an "exceptional and overriding power," it must be used sparingly, with caution, and only in special and extraordinary situations.

In **Mathai @ Jobyvs George &Anr,**[22] a Constitution Bench of the Supreme Court deliberated on a matter referred to them by a division bench of the same Court. The Division Bench had considered narrowing the scope of accepting cases under Article 136 that fell into the following categories:

i. All matters involving a substantial question of law relating to the interpretation of the Constitution of India.
ii. All matters of national or public importance.
iii. Validity of laws: Central and State.
iv. After KesavanandaBharti,the judicial review of Constitutional Amendments
v. To settle differences of opinion on important issues of law between High Courts
vi. Cases where the Court is satisfied that there has been a grave miscarriage of justice
vii. Where there is a prima facie violation of the Fundamental Right of a person.

However, the constitutional bench refused to limit the scope of article 136, stating that no attempt should be made to limit the court's authority under the article. Furthermore, it was said that "in the interest of justice, we believe it would be better to use the said power with caution rather than limit the power conferred"

The Court has strengthened the principle of applying Article 136 in "exceptional" cases over the years. In **AshishChadha v. AshaKumari,**[23] the Court stated quite clearly that "though the discretionary power vested in this Court under Article 136 is not subject to any limitations, it must be used sparingly and in exceptional cases". Thus, it is clear that the firm determination of the Judges alone will make a change in entertaining the petition under Art. 136.

From **Pritam Singh v. The State** to **Mathai @ Joby v. George**, the Supreme Court has repeatedly emphasized the importance of exercising discretionary power under Article 136 consistently and judiciously.[24]

CHAPTER SIX

CONCLUSION

The Supreme Court of India grants Special Leave to Appeal at its discretion. There are no regulations governing when the Supreme Court may exercise its discretion.[1] The discretion is usually exercised by the Supreme Court only in special and extraordinary situations where legal issues require immediate attention or where a question of law on general public importance arises.

Article 136, no doubt, specifies that the Supreme Court may, in its discretion, grant special permission to appeal from any judgment, decree, determination, sentence, or order passed or made by any court or tribunal in the territory of India. However, it is not specified in Article 136 of the Constitution in what circumstances the aforementioned discretion should be exercised. The increase in special leave petitions filed with the Supreme Court places a significant burden on its docket and contributes to the judicial backlog; therefore, the Supreme Court must exercise greater restraint and judicial discipline, limiting the invocation of this extraordinary jurisdiction under Article 136 to rare cases.